Copyright © 2011 XAMonline, Inc.
All rights reserved. No part of the material protected by this copyright notice may be reproduced or utilized in any form or by any means, electronic or mechanical, including photocopying, recording or by any information storage and retrievable system, without written permission from the copyright holder.

To obtain permission(s) to use the material from this work for any purpose including workshops or seminars, please submit a written request to:

> XAMonline, Inc.
> 25 First Street, Suite 106
> Cambridge, MA 02141
> Toll Free: 1-800-509-4128
> Email: info@xamonline.com
> Web: www.xamonline.com
> Fax: 1-617-583-5552

Library of Congress Cataloging-in-Publication Data

Wynne, Sharon A.
    NYSTCE ATS-W Secondary Assessment of Teaching Skills- Written 91 Practice Test 1: Teacher Certification / Sharon A. Wynne. -1st ed.
    ISBN: 978-1-60787-225-2
    1. NYSTCE ATS-W Secondary Assessment of Teaching Skills- Written 91 Practice Test 1   2. Study Guides   3. NYSTCE
    4. Teachers' Certification & Licensure   5. Careers

Disclaimer:
The opinions expressed in this publication are the sole works of XAMonline and were created independently from the National Education Association, Educational Testing Service, or any State Department of Education, National Evaluation Systems or other testing affiliates.

Between the time of publication and printing, state specific standards as well as testing formats and website information may change that is not included in part or in whole within this product. Sample test questions are developed by XAMonline and reflect similar content as on real tests; however, they are not former tests. XAMonline assembles content that aligns with state standards but makes no claims nor guarantees teacher candidates a passing score. Numerical scores are determined by testing companies such as NES or ETS and then are compared with individual state standards. A passing score varies from state to state.

Printed in the United States of America   œ-1
NYSTCE ATS-W Secondary Assessment of Teaching Skills- Written 91 Practice Test 1
ISBN: 978-1-60787-225-2

NYSTCE ATS-W PRE TEST

1. **Which of the following activities would best suit a group of 6th grade students in order to promote classroom participation?**

   A. Students read a selection independently, highlight important aspects of the article, write a one sentence summary of what they've read, share the summary out loud in front of the whole class.

   B. A pair of students brainstorm ideas to activate their prior knowledge about a topic, they read a selection independently highlighting important information, a small group of students work to create a one sentence summary, and then share their ideas out with the whole class.

   C. Students partner read a selection about a certain topic, and then think of their own follow-up activity.

   D. Students are given a list of vocabulary words they will encounter in their reading and with a partner they use a dictionary to look up each word's definition, and then student's share, with the class, a way that each word applies to their own life.

2. **A first grade teacher is having a difficult time with her class. They are very attentive in the morning when they first arrive and work nicely at their seats. However, in the afternoon students seem to be squirming and moving. She cannot understand why they can't just sit still and do their work quietly. What might the problem be?**

   A. The students need to have a snack during the latter part of the morning.

   B. The students are not being given enough time for recess.

   C. The teacher needs to incorporate more activities that allow the students to move.

   D. The teacher must have been given a class full of students who have ADHD.

3. **Teachers should plan lessons based on**

   A. What the children are most interested in learning about.

   B. Activities that will engage students and increase student achievement.

   C. State standardized testing criteria.

   D. Objective-driven learning activities.

4. Middle school students have the ability to process greater amounts of information than elementary school children. Which stage of development does this fall under?

   A. Cognitive

   B. Linguistic

   C. Social

   D. Moral

5. A new 7th grade teacher is planning a Social Studies lesson about Native Americans. His lesson should include:

   A. Physical movement.

   B. Group conversation.

   C. Lecture material and note taking.

   D. All of the above.

6. Margaret, an 8th grade social studies teacher has been teaching for over 20 years. She has always used lecture as her primary method of teaching. Margaret's principal has suggested that she try other methods of instruction. What is something that Margaret could try that would be the most effective?

   A. Margaret can add some visual aids like maps and graphs to her lectures.

   B. Margaret could have the students use two-column notes.

   C. Margaret needs to have students engaged in an activity that connects the content she wishes to teach with students' lives.

   D. Margaret should have some guest speakers come into the classroom.

7. **Miss Appleby is planning a lesson about the American Presidents for her 2nd graders. Her plan is to tell the students facts about Abraham Lincoln and George Washington. She plans to talk to them for about 45 minutes. What can Miss Appleby do to improve this lesson?**

   A. Talk to them and give them facts for a shorter amount of time.

   B. Break the lecture into two days; talk about Lincoln one day and Washington another.

   C. Have the students take notes while she is teaching.

   D. Break the lesson into two days and include a few objective-driven learning activities.

8. **What is an advantage of using alternative assessments?**

   A. They can be graded quickly and students will get immediate feedback.

   B. They are easier for students to study for.

   C. They are more authentic and give the teacher a greater read on student learning.

   D. They do not include tricky multiple choice or true false questions.

9. **A teacher always assesses her students by having them write a short essay response to a question. There are five students who seem to be doing well in class but have failed each of their tests. What should the teacher do?**

   A. The teacher needs to vary the way she is assessing the students. Perhaps these five students are not very good writers and are not able to effectively communicate their knowledge through an essay.

   B. The teacher needs to have extra help sessions for these five students because it is obvious that they are having difficulties with the content being presented in class.

   C. The teacher doesn't need to do anything. The students need to study harder for the tests and take their time.

   D. The teacher should take the time to develop, and teach a lesson, on note taking in class and study skills at home.

10. An English teacher had students find the lyrics to their favorite song and print them from the computer. She then had students find examples of figurative language using those lyrics. Every student in her class passed the test when she gave it. What is the best explanation for this?

    A. The teacher must have been voted teacher of the year for the previous year.

    B. The teacher obviously has a bright group of students and simply "got lucky".

    C. The teacher's lesson was child centered and she made the lesson relevant to their own lives so the students took a vested interest in the learning.

    D. The teacher must have given the students the answers beforehand.

11. How is a K-W-L chart a child-centered learning activity?

    A. The students need to think about what they already know about a topic.

    B. The students need to think of a topic they don't know everything about already.

    C. It builds on the natural curiosity of children because it makes them think about what they want to learn/know about a topic.

    D. It is a graphic organizer that the students need to fill in with their own information.

12. **A teacher wants to plan a lesson about magnets that her students will really enjoy and become engaged in. Which is the best thing to include in her planning?**

    A. Use a K-W-L chart to activate students' prior knowledge, determine what they are interested in learning, and allowing them to research the answers to their questions prior to filling in the 'Learned' section of the chart.

    B. Allow students to "play" with the magnets before any learning objectives are taught.

    C. Reading a book about magnets before any hands-on work is started.

    D. She should plan a field trip to a science museum so the students can have experiences with magnets first hand from a science expert.

13. **When planning a lesson, why is it a good idea to think in terms of before, during, and after learning activities and objectives?**

    A. It keeps the lesson moving at a good pace for the students.

    B. Students activate their background knowledge, are then actively engaged in learning, and then are assessed on what they are able to produce.

    C. The teacher is given three distinct areas to assess student understanding.

    D. It makes planning a lesson much easier for the teacher.

14. **Why is it necessary to activate student's background knowledge before introducing a new topic?**

    A. Students will learn better if they can attach a new concept onto something concrete that is already in their background knowledge.

    B. It ensures that students aren't daydreaming about something else when a new concept is being taught.

    C. It keeps students on task during the active learning stage of a lesson.

    D. Students will learn best when a new topic is relevant to their own lives and that is why we activate background knowledge.

15. **Mark is planning a social studies lesson for his high school freshman on the 1920s. What would be the best activity for Mark to use to begin his lesson?**

    A. Students should read a short article about that includes the highlights of the 1920s.

    B. Students should work in small groups and brainstorm all the things they already know about the 1920s.

    C. Students should research a few key topics of the 1920s.

    D. Students should be introduced to some key vocabulary that is important in understanding the 1920s.

16. **Mr. Henderson wants his students to know exactly what "comprehension" is so they can understand that when they read, they are not just reading the words, but understanding what the text is saying. What should Mr. Henderson do?**

    A. Have students look up the word comprehension, write down its definition, and write a sentence explaining how comprehension and reading go together.

    B. He should have students write an essay about what comprehension is and why it is important in reading.

    C. Have students complete a word map for the word comprehension where they write its definition, determine some synonyms and antonyms, and determine three ways that they know it has occurred.

    D. Complete an acrostic poem using the word comprehension.

17. **What is the purpose of using clustering or mind mapping activities in a lesson?**

    A. It helps students become more organized.

    B. Mind mapping and clustering is a great study skill that students can extend to their own independent study habits.

    C. It helps students organize large quantities of information in a visual or tactile-kinesthetic way.

    D. Mind mapping shows a teacher visually what a student is thinking mentally.

18. **What might be an explanation for why young children under the age of 2 put everything their mouths?**

    A. They are developing their sense of taste and they have not developed the knowledge that only food goes in your mouth.
    B. Their vocabulary develops faster if they are able to utilize the tongue muscle in various ways.
    C. Piaget says that children from birth to 2 are in the sensory motor stage and this is how children experience the world.
    D. Only kinesthetic-tactile learners do this. It is an early indicator of what type of learner a child will be.

19. A young child in first grade is a struggling reader. What should the teacher do?

    A. Refer the child for special education testing; she must have a learning disability.

    B. Continue to instruct the child at her instructional reading level. Learning is developmental and she may just not be developmentally where the other children are.

    C. Continue to monitor the student and pass her observations onto the second grade teacher next year.

    D. Have a discussion with the parents about what they should be doing at home to increase the student's reading achievements.

20. Mrs. Talmadge does not like her students to talk while they are working. She believes that the best learning occurs in a quiet, focused, on-task environment. She does not allow students to work cooperatively or in pairs. Students only complete learning activities individually. What does Mrs. Talmadge need to understand about the brain and how it best learns?

    A. The brain is social.

    B. The brain is a complex adaptive system.

    C. We use patterns to learn more effectively.

    D. Emotions are crucial to developing patterns.

21. At first glance it would appear that Ms. Marshall does not know how to manage her classroom because students in her class are standing over their desks, or tapping their pencils on their legs, and walking around the room at times. However, upon further examination, it is clear that Ms. Marshall's students are all on task and actively engaged in their learning. Ms. Marshal must embrace

    A. The constructivist approach to learning

    B. The multiple intelligence theory of interpersonal learning.

    C. The multiple intelligence theory of bodily/kinesthetic learning.

    D. The latest brain research and its importance toward learning.

22. In which subject would students do much better if they were able to connect the learning to their own interests?

    A. Physical Education

    B. Math

    C. Writing

    D. All of the above

23. A 3rd grade teacher wants to integrate more critical thinking lessons into her day. Which of the lessons below will best incorporate critical thinking skills?

    A. Doing some comparative shopping to find the better deal; 30% off each item purchased, or perhaps buy one get one free of a more expensive item.

    B. Writing how-to directions that students will then follow.

    C. Taking a field trip to reinforce what has been learned in the classroom.

    D. Brainstorming a list of newly learned concepts.

24. Which is the best example of a question that would be part of the synthesis segment on Bloom's Taxonomy?

    A. When did Christopher Columbus set sail for the new world?

    B. How might Christopher Columbus' journey be different if it were to take place today?

    C. Which explorer do you think had the greatest impact on life as we know it today? Why?

    D. What were the names of Columbus' three ships?

25. Bradley, a 10th grade student, has recently been getting poor grades in his English class. Bradley has always been a straight A student but is now receiving Cs and Ds consistently. What might be going on with Bradley?

   A. Bradley probably needs glasses because he cannot see the words as easily as he used to be able to.

   B. Bradley no longer likes his English teacher and is doing poorly.

   C. Bradley has been playing basketball and it started a few months ago.

   D. Bradley probably has something going on at home like a divorce or neglect.

26. A teacher has a list of classroom rules posted that she made up prior to the beginning of the school year. She has reviewed them with the class, but they are having a difficult time following the rules that have been posted. What might the problem be?

   A. The teacher must have a class full of students who have been diagnosed with ADHD.

   B. The students did not participate in putting the list of rules together so they do not feel any ownership of the expectations.

   C. The teacher didn't put the correct rules on her chart.

   D. The students don't know where the classroom rules are posted so they are unable to refer to them as needed.

27. **Which would be an activity that might be seen in the success-oriented classroom?**

    A. A teacher has students working in collaborative pairs completing a Venn Diagram comparing two versions of the fairy tale *Cinderella*.

    B. Students are taking a multiple-choice test.

    C. A teacher is lecturing and students are diligently taking notes.

    D. Each student is reading a fairy tale and then they will discuss the differences between each story in small groups.

28. **A well-prepared reading lesson will include**

    A. lecture, note taking, and a quiz or test.

    B. a before, during, and after reading activity

    C. independent reading, paired reading, and independent seatwork

    D. a whole group activity based on a shared novel that everyone can discuss.

29. **A kindergarten teacher evaluates a student's social skills while a student is in the writing center, at the play center, at a math center, and out on the playground for two weeks. Which method of social skill assessment is the teacher using?**

    A. Sociometric measures

    B. Teacher rating

    C. Role play

    D. Direct observation

30. **Mr. Anderson plays kickball with his class every Friday at recess. What important skill is Mr. Anderson teaching his students during this time?**

    A. A great math lesson on how to keep score.

    B. A physics lesson on the trajectory of the ball when kicked a certain way.

    C. The value of being on a team and playing together fairly.

    D. How to follow directions to play a fair game.

31. A teacher has 85 middle school students that she is responsible for. She has a bin for each of her classes that she calls the "done bin". This management strategy most likely

    A. Does not help students because they want to hand their papers to the teacher directly.

    B. Allows students to look at each other's papers.

    C. Distracting to students because they forget to put their papers in the correct bin.

    D. helpful to students because they always know where to put their papers when they have completed their work

32. Before lunch a teacher lines her classroom up by the row that they sit in. This is an example of

    A. a proactive strategy

    B. a transitional interference

    C. a waste of time and inefficient

    D. a transition signal

33. When a fourth grade teacher wants to get the attention of her students, she raises her hand and smiles. Students then do the same when they notice her until everyone in the class is doing the same thing. This is an example of

    A. a proactive strategy

    B. a transition signal

    C. a waste of time that students will not understand

    D. a transitional interference

34. A teacher's room is so cold one day that her classes must take place in a different location for the day. What is something that the teacher should take a few moments to do?

    A. Tell kids to wear warmer clothes tomorrow in case their room is just as cold the next day.

    B. Put a note on her regular classroom door indicating where they are for the day.

    C. Report the problem to maintenance and have them fix the temperature gauge immediately.

    D. Become familiar with the evacuation routes for this particular room and share these plans with the students.

35. A state's curriculum says that in the first quarter students should learn summarizing, making connections to text, and using context clues while reading. This is the

    A. scope

    B. sequence

    C. outline

    D. curriculum alignment

36. At the beginning of each school year it is a good idea for the teacher to

    A. use the exit tests from the prior year to determine the abilities of their new students.

    B. place students in groups and evaluate how they do and rearrange groups accordingly.

    C. give a diagnostic assessment to determine students' abilities.

    D. talk to their student's prior year teachers to determine their ability levels.

37. A teacher is teaching time to her second grade students. The best way that she can differentiate is to

    A. teach one group time, one group multiplication, and one group division.

    B. have one group use technology to learn time and the other to use paper pencil method.

    C. break students into groups and have them all complete the same task.

    D. determine which students need practice with time to the various hours, which group needs time to the 5 minutes, and which group needs to learn time to the minute.

38. Students are given a choice between 3 final projects to complete after reading a group novel. How has the teacher chosen to differentiate?

    A. Product

    B. Process

    C. Content

    D. This is not an example of differentiation.

39. A 10th grade teacher has presented her class of sophomores with a scientific scenario dealing with a problem in their school that they must solve. Four groups have been given different, but related scenarios to discuss. The teacher has

    A. Differentiated instruction

    B. Used cooperative learning models

    C. Provided a relevant learning experience

    D. All of the above

40. What does the quote, "Assessment drives instruction," mean?

    A. Assessment must be a part of every instructional model.

    B. The results of any given assessment should be the determining factors of the next step of instruction.

    C. Standardized assessment test results should drive the foundation for the development of curriculum.

    D. Different methods of assessment should be used to vary presentation of material to students.

41. A teacher wants to give her students a pretest before teaching them fractions so that she can plan her instruction effectively and group students according to their ability. What kind of assessment should the teacher give as a pretest?

    A. A project based assessment.

    B. An anecdotal record.

    C. A formal test

    D. A portfolio assessment

42. An English teacher needs to determine certain reading behaviors that her students possess. Which is the best type of assessment for her to give?

    A. Anecdotal records.

    B. Formal standardized tests

    C. Rating scale or checklist.

    D. Portfolio assessment

43. A teacher wants to know her student's feelings about a project they just completed; each student needed to create a commercial about their favorite book that they had read as a class. Which is the best method of assessment for the teacher to use?

    A. Standardized test

    B. Portfolio assessment

    C. Rating scale and checklist

    D. Questioning

44. How can questioning be used as a powerful assessment tool?

    A. The students answer questions that are generated by the teacher.

    B. The students generate assessment questions to ask each other.

    C. The teacher questions students and collects a lot of valuable information.

    D. Open ended written questions will tell a teacher a lot more about student knowledge than will oral questioning.

45. Kellough and Roberts feel that students should be evaluated on

    A. What the learner says

    B. What the learner does

    C. What the learner.

    D. All of the above.

46. What is the best method for teaching social skills within the classroom?

    A. Standardized testing

    B. Heterogeneous grouping methods

    C. Teacher role modeling

    D. Student role playing

47. A second grade teacher has four reading groups named after various birds. This teacher uses

    A. group fragmentation

    B. management transition

    C. transition signals

    D. seat work

48. **Which teacher probably has an easier time managing her students' transitions?**

    A. A teacher whose daily schedule is different every day.

    B. A teacher who tells her students what to expect each day.

    C. A teacher whose daily schedule is consistent each day.

    D. A teacher who has taught elementary school before and now teacher middle school.

49. **Which of the following does not factor into invitational learning?**

    A. A well lit classroom.

    B. A temperature controlled classroom.

    C. A calming atmosphere.

    D. Proximity to resource classrooms and the cafeteria.

50. **What is the proper way to prepare for a tornado?**

    A. Have students remain at their seats with their heads down.

    B. Have students clear of any windows and have them crouch down on the floor and cover their heads with their hands.

    C. Exit outside using the closest exits.

    D. All students should convene in the gymnasium until any dangerous weather has passed.

51. **It is necessary for 4th grade students to learn multiplication and division before they can be introduced to reducing fractions. This criteria is known as the curriculum**

    A. Sequence

    B. Scope

    C. Design

    D. Instruction

52. **What is the best reason for giving a pre-test in math?**

    A. The teacher needs to let the students know what they are going to learn about in an upcoming unit.

    B. The teacher needs to know if students are ready to learn new material.

    C. It will help the teacher differentiate instruction during the unit.

    D. You can compare students' prior knowledge to how they do on the final assessment.

53. **A teacher makes a final exam for her English Literature class that includes some multiple choice and short answer questions. What type of assessment has the teacher created?**

    A. A formal test

    B. An informal test

    C. An anecdotal record

    D. A portfolio assessment

54. **As a form of assessment to use on her report cards, a teacher keeps notes on observed behaviors of her students during guided reading groups. What type of assessment is this an example of?**

    A. Formal assessment

    B. Informal assessment

    C. Portfolio assessment

    D. Anecdotal records

55. **A student and a teacher are sitting down together and deciding which pieces of student work to keep to document the student's progress. This is an example of which type of assessment?**

    A. Rating scales and checklists

    B. Anecdotal records

    C. Portfolio assessment

    D. Questioning

56. **Which assessment tool gives teachers a great deal of information on a daily basis?**

    A. Questioning

    B. Anecdotal records

    C. Formal assessments

    D. Portfolio assessments

57. **Why might a school use Criterion-referenced assessments?**

    A. To make sure that the content schools are teaching students applies to real-world needs.

    B. To document and measure whether schools are making AYP (Annual Yearly Progress) as documented in No Child Left Behind.

    C. To rank students for differentiated instruction within the school.

    D. To rate schools for state funding.

58. **Why might a school use Norm-referenced assessments?**

    A. To make sure that the content schools are teaching students applies to real world needs.

    B. To document and measure whether schools are making AYP (Annual Yearly Progress) as documented in No Child Left Behind.

    C. To rank students for differentiated instruction within the school.

    D. To rate schools for state funding.

59. **The DRA is a direct reading assessment tool used by many schools across the country. Teachers listen to students read and determine the miscues they are making while they read, but it also asks the student to use reading strategies and read strategically for comprehension. What type of assessment is the DRA?**

    A. Summative assessment

    B. Placement assessment

    C. Interest and attitude assessment

    D. Diagnostic assessment

60. **Two fourth grade teachers share students for math. Before each unit of study each teacher gives her class a pretest. What type of assessment is this?**

    A. Readiness assessment

    B. Interest and attitude assessment

    C. Evaluation assessment

    D. Placement assessment

61. **What was the purpose of the No Child Left Behind Act passed in 2001?**

    A. It was an act passed as a way to ensure that all children passed a standardized assessment before being passed on to the next grade.

    B. To mandate a set amount of funds to schools that did a good job of educating their students.

    C. It aims to improve schools by increasing educational standards and holds schools, school districts, and states accountable for performance and progress of students.

    D. It allows parents to choose which school their child attends by using vouchers.

62. **What are magnet schools?**

    A. Schools that attract a certain demographic of student.

    B. Schools that are built around the regular education building.

    C. Schools that are available for any student within the district. These schools usually have a theme.

    D. Schools that are not run by the school districts but take money, based on student enrollment, from the local public school.

63. **There are many professional organizations for teachers to join in New York state at the local or national level. What is the advantage of teachers joining a professional organization?**

    A. It is a great way for teachers to become well-known in their field.

    B. Joining a professional organization is a great way to reduce a teacher's tax base.

    C. Professional organizations are the only way to get up-to-date teaching information about a discipline because state organizations have better information than the districts do.

    D. By joining a professional organization, a teacher can network with other educators outside of their own school or district and gain valuable teaching ideas and information.

64. **Math teachers K-8 in a district are using the same math program from the same publisher. How was this decision most likely made?**

    A. K-8 teachers got together and looked over several different math programs/models and decided that the one they are using is the best one to use.

    B. Most likely it was a centralized decision by the district central office and the math program was used to ensure consistency across grades K-8.

    C. Parents of the district got together and decided that the math program the district is using is the best one for their children.

    D. Each individual school decided to use the current math program because it was the best one for their individual schools.

65. **What is the responsibility of the New York State Board of Regents?**

    A. This group is the chief officer of the school district,

    B. A sixteen member group that presides over the NYSED and develops guidelines, creates and monitors aid, and develops policies.

    C. It is a collective bargaining organization.

    D. It allows small school districts to combine their financial power to share costs.

66. **A teacher has just finished teaching a lesson about the branches of government. As she is reviewing the grades of her students for the unit, she is also reviewing what worked well and didn't work well. What is the teacher doing when she asks herself these questions?**

    A. Grading the students.

    B. Deciding if the unit is worth teaching next year.

    C. Self-assessing and reflecting on how to improve her teaching the next time she teaches the unit.

    D. Determining the content that needs to be added to the unit next time in order for her students to master the material.

67. A science teacher realizes that one of his weaknesses is showing his students how to read the textbook to improve understanding. What is something the teacher might consider doing?

    A. He should take a course on science and the standardized testing methods used to evaluate students in his state.

    B. He should attend some professional development opportunities that address teaching students to comprehend non-fiction text.

    C. He should speak with the English teacher on his team and have them work a little more with comprehending non-fiction material.

    D. He should find a textbook that is below the students' grade level that they can easily understand and focus on the content rather than the decoding while they read.

68. A local middle school English grade level department meets every Wednesday with their subject matter peers. They call this meeting a PLC (Primary Learning Community). What is most likely the purpose of these PLCs?

    A. The PLC allows teachers to learn from each other and share successful lessons they have used in their classrooms.

    B. It is a chance for teachers review and change student's IEPs.

    C. PLCs are the first step before a CST meeting.

    D. The meeting gives these teachers a chance to review curriculum and discuss changes that must be made to meet the needs of their students.

69. A new 4th grade teacher has been hired and this is her first year teaching. What is the best thing that the district or school can do to make this teacher's first year successful?

   A. Have this new hire attend an orientation that will orient the new teacher to the practices and policies of the county.

   B. Supply her with several books about being a new teacher and what other teachers have done to successfully make it through the first year.

   C. Observe her classroom more often than a veteran teacher and offer constructive criticism on ways to improve instruction and management within her classroom and make reports to central office on her performance.

   D. Assign a mentor teacher to her so she can ask for professional teaching advice in the areas she is struggling in.

70. It is the second month of school and a teacher has received several emails from one parent in particular. What should the teacher do?

   A. Ignore the parent's contacts that are not well justified.

   B. Do everything the parent suggests. After all, the parent knows their child better than the teacher.

   C. Respond politely to the parent telling them that she will take their thoughts into consideration and consult with their mentor teacher about how to handle the situation.

   D. Alert the principal and have them meet with the parent so that they will stop harassing the teacher.

71. A 2nd grade parent complains to a teacher that he does not feel that the teacher is communicating well with the parents. What is one way that the teacher can increase communication with her students' parents?

   A. The teacher can send a weekly newsletter informing parents of the classroom activities for that week and the week to come.

   B. The teacher can call parents of children who were difficult that week or had a great week.

   C. The teacher can invite parents into the classroom to help out more often.

   D. The teacher can invite parents to holiday parties so that they feel they are a part of the classroom.

72. A teacher is having a conference with a parent tomorrow. She has records of student behavior and has the notes that she has been keeping about the child's classroom behaviors and performance. What else would be helpful for the teacher to have handy before the conference?

   A. The principal should also attend to give the teacher support.

   B. Another grade level teacher should attend to give the teacher support.

   C. The child should also be at the conference so they can defend their position.

   D. Samples of student work and models of exemplary work should be available to support the teacher's position.

73. What is one of the benefits of having students work with an adult mentor?

    A. The student will learn how to be a mature, responsible adult.

    B. The student will learn about diversity and respect for their elders.

    C. The student is exposed to multicultural education and feels a sense of personalized instruction.

    D. It takes some of the responsibility of education off the teacher's and parent's shoulders. After all, it takes a village.

74. Mrs. Montgory's class has several students who are reading below grade level. However, the families of these students also cannot afford to have a private tutor. Mrs. Montgory cannot give any more time to help these students individually. What would be the best solution to help these struggling students receive more individualized attention?

    A. Mrs. Montgory can pay for the private tutor herself.

    B. The librarian can work with the students individually during library time each week.

    C. Mrs. Montgory can work with retired community members to come in and read with students a few times a week on a volunteer basis.

    D. The parents must be given a strict schedule to follow at home in order to assist with improving their child's reading.

75. **What will students gain by having community members involved in the classroom and the school?**

    A. Students will learn how to interact with adults.

    B. Students will experience accountability and responsibility.

    C. Students will see what it is like to be a community leader.

    D. Students will learn to set goals to improve their performance in school with adult intervention.

76. **What is usually the teacher's role when a student has been referred to a CST for evaluation?**

    A. The work is extensive for a teacher because they are given strict guidelines to follow within the classroom over several weeks.

    B. Teachers are asked to make observations and report to the team in about a week.

    C. There is usually a little paperwork for teachers to fill out and some in-class observations of a student.

    D. The classroom teacher doesn't have any responsibility. Referring and evaluating a student is the specialists' responsibility.

77. **Does a parent have to be involved in a child's IEP?**

    A. Yes

    B. No

    C. Only under certain circumstances.

    D. It is optional.

78. **What is the least restrictive environment under IDEA?**

    A. A law that says that disabled students can not be restrained by teachers or assistants.

    B. The mandate that children be educated to the maximum extent appropriate with their non-disabled peers.

    C. A modification that sometimes appears in student's IEPs.

    D. A policy where disabled students can be placed in the regular classroom, as long as such placement does not interfere with the student's educational plan.

79. **What is mainstreaming?**

    A. A policy where disabled students can be placed in the regular classroom, as long as such placement does not interfere with the student's educational plan.

    B. A law that says that disabled students can not be restrained by teachers or assistants.

    C. A way of teaching in the classroom that ensures that all students are taught the same way across the curriculum.

    D. The mandate that children be educated to the maximum extent appropriate with their non-disabled peers.

80. **A teacher has a student that wears the same dirty sweatshirt to class each day, never has a lunch, and claims that he lives in a closet. What should the teacher do?**

    A. Nothing.

    B. Be the best teacher she can to this poor student.

    C. Report the potential neglect situation to authorities; she is mandated by law to.

    D. See if she has any clothes at home that would fit this student and pass them on to him.

ANSWER KEY

1. B	28. B	55. C
2. C	29. D	56. A
3. D	30. C	57. B
4. A	31. D	58. C
5. D	32. A	59. D
6. C	33. B	60. D
7. D	34. D	61. C
8. C	35. B	62. C
9. A	36. C	63. D
10. C	37. D	64. B
11. C	38. A	65. B
12. A	39. D	66. C
13. B	40. B	67. B
14. A	41. C	68. A
15. B	42. A	69. D
16. C	43. C	70. C
17. C	44. C	71. A
18. C	45. D	72. D
19. B	46. C	73. C
20. A	47. A	74. C
21. C	48. C	75. B
22. D	49. D	76. C
23. A	50. B	77. A
24. B	51. A	78. B
25. D	52. C	79. A
26. B	53. B	80. C
27. A	54. D	

RATIONALES

1. **Which of the following activities would best suit a group of 6th grade students in order to promote classroom participation?**

   A. Students read a selection independently, highlight important aspects of the article, write a one sentence summary of what they've read, share the summary out loud in front of the whole class.

   B. A pair of students brainstorm ideas to activate their prior knowledge about a topic, they read a selection independently highlighting important information, a small group of students work to create a one sentence summary, and then share their ideas out with the whole class.

   C. Students partner read a selection about a certain topic, and then think of their own follow-up activity.

   D. Students are given a list of vocabulary words they will encounter in their reading and with a partner they use a dictionary to look up each word's definition, and then student's share, with the class, a way that each word applies to their own life.

   Answer B: In this scenario, students have several opportunities to work together to first brainstorm ideas so that when they are asked to share them with the whole class, they feel comfortable with what they have come up with as a team.

2. **A first grade teacher is having a difficult time with her class. They are very attentive in the morning when they first arrive and work nicely at their seats. However, in the afternoon students seem to be squirming and moving. She cannot understand why they can't just sit still and do their work quietly. What might the problem be?**

   A. The students need to have a snack during the latter part of the morning.

   B. The students are not being given enough time for recess.

   C. The teacher needs to incorporate more activities that allow the students to move.

   D. The teacher must have been given a class full of students who have ADHD.

   Answer C: Young children need opportunities to move throughout the day. Having them move from one area of the room to another several times during instructional times is a way to get students up and moving.

3. **Teachers should plan lessons based on**

    A. What the children are most interested in learning about.

    B. Activities that will engage students and increase student achievement.

    C. State standardized testing criteria.

    D. Objective-driven learning activities.

    Answer D: By planning lessons focusing on objectives, it ensures that students will learn what is mandated by the curriculum. It also helps give teachers a focus while they are planning their lessons to ensure that they do not get off track.

4. **Middle school students have the ability to process greater amounts of information than elementary school children. Which stage of development does this fall under?**

    A. Cognitive

    B. Linguistic

    C. Social

    D. Moral

    Answer A: As we move through childhood into adulthood, our cognitive abilities increase. Therefore, middle school students are able to process greater amounts of information than elementary school children and adults are able to process more than middle school children.

5. **A new 7th grade teacher is planning a Social Studies lesson about Native Americans. His lesson should include:**

    A. Physical movement.

    B. Group conversation.

    C. Lecture material and note taking.

    D. All of the above.

    Answer D: By including more modalities of learning, students are able to learn and retain information better. When students converse with each other they hear and think about other students' ideas. Lecture and note taking should also be part of some lessons because students need to have some information given to them.

6. **Margaret, an 8th grade social studies teacher has been teaching for over 20 years. She has always used lecture as her primary method of teaching. Margaret's principal has suggested that she try other methods of instruction. What is something that Margaret could try that would be the most effective?**

   A. Margaret can add some visual aids like maps and graphs to her lectures.

   B. Margaret could have the students use two-column notes.

   C. Margaret needs to have students engaged in an activity that connects the content she wishes to teach with students' lives.

   D. Margaret should have some guest speakers come into the classroom.

   Answer C: When something is relevant to our lives, we connect with it better. Children are no different. If instructional material is relevant to their own lives, they will connect with it better and learn it. In addition, if students are actively engaged with the material and can actively work with it, they will take more ownership in their learning.

7. **Miss Appleby is planning a lesson about the American Presidents for her 2nd graders. Her plan is to tell the students facts about Abraham Lincoln and George Washington. She plans to talk to them for about 45 minutes. What can Miss Appleby do to improve this lesson?**

   A. Talk to them and give them facts for a shorter amount of time.

   B. Break the lecture into two days; talk about Lincoln one day and Washington another.

   C. Have the students take notes while she is teaching.

   D. Break the lesson into two days and include a few objective-driven learning activities.

   Answer D: Students at this age need many activities over a 45-minute period. Mrs. Appleby should teach one president each day and each day, have several hands-on activities in order for the students to be engaged in their learning.

8. **What is an advantage of using alternative assessments?**

    A. They can be graded quickly and students will get immediate feedback.

    B. They are easier for students to study for.

    C. They are more authentic and give the teacher a greater read on student learning.

    D. They do not include tricky multiple choice or true false questions.

    Answer C: Alternative assessments are not standardized and are a better measure of what students really know and what they have truly mastered.

9. **A teacher always assesses her students by having them write a short essay response to a question. There are five students who seem to be doing well in class but have failed each of their tests. What should the teacher do?**

    A. The teacher needs to vary the way she is assessing the students. Perhaps these five students are not very good writers and are not able to effectively communicate their knowledge through an essay.

    B. The teacher needs to have extra help sessions for these five students because it is obvious that they are having difficulties with the content being presented in class.

    C. The teacher doesn't need to do anything. The students need to study harder for the tests and take their time.

    D. The teacher should take the time to develop, and teach a lesson, on note taking in class and study skills at home.

    Answer A: Although many believe that short answer responses are a great way to get accurate information about what students have mastered on an assessment, it also measures how well students can write. For some students writing is a challenge and they do not want to do it therefore, their responses may not accurately measure what they have mastered.

10. **An English teacher had students find the lyrics to their favorite song and print them from the computer. She then had students find examples of figurative language using those lyrics. Every student in her class passed the test when she gave it. What is the best explanation for this?**

    A. The teacher must have been voted teacher of the year for the previous year.

    B. The teacher obviously has a bright group of students and simply "got lucky".

    C. The teacher's lesson was child centered and she made the lesson relevant to their own lives so the students took a vested interest in the learning.

    D. The teacher must have given the students the answers beforehand.

    Answer C: Any child centered activity that is relevant to their own lives will get the students more involved and usually bring about a greater degree of learning and mastery.

11. **How is a K-W-L chart a child-centered learning activity?**

    A. The students need to think about what they already know about a topic.

    B. The students need to think of a topic they don't know everything about already.

    C. It builds on the natural curiosity of children because it makes them think about what they want to learn/know about a topic.

    D. It is a graphic organizer that the students need to fill in with their own information.

    Answer C: The K stands for, "What we know", the W stands for "What we want to find out or learn", and the L stands for "What we have learned". Because students contribute to what they want they are interested in learning, the activity is a child-centered activity.

12. **A teacher wants to plan a lesson about magnets that her students will really enjoy and become engaged in. Which is the best thing to include in her planning?**

    A. Use a K-W-L chart to activate students' prior knowledge, determine what they are interested in learning, and allowing them to research the answers to their questions prior to filling in the 'Learned' section of the chart.

    B. Allow students to "play" with the magnets before any learning objectives are taught.

    C. Reading a book about magnets before any hands-on work is started.

    D. She should plan a field trip to a science museum so the students can have experiences with magnets first hand from a science expert.

    Answer A: By using a K-W-L chart, the teacher has helped to activate students' background knowledge. She then has students generate a list of things they are interested in learning about and then allows the students time to find or research the answers to those questions.

13. **When planning a lesson, why is it a good idea to think in terms of before, during, and after learning activities and objectives?**

    A. It keeps the lesson moving at a good pace for the students.

    B. Students activate their background knowledge, are then actively engaged in learning, and then are assessed on what they are able to produce.

    C. The teacher is given three distinct areas to assess student understanding.

    D. It makes planning a lesson much easier for the teacher.

    Answer B: In order for students to learn well, they should have their background knowledge activated in a before learning activity. Students will be actively engaged in a learning activity where the teacher is available to assist and guide students in their independent learning. Afterward, the students show the teacher through assessment what they have learned.

14. **Why is it necessary to activate student's background knowledge before introducing a new topic?**

    A. Students will learn better if they can attach a new concept onto something concrete that is already in their background knowledge.

    B. It ensures that students aren't daydreaming about something else when a new concept is being taught.

    C. It keeps students on task during the active learning stage of a lesson.

    D. Students will learn best when a new topic is relevant to their own lives and that is why we activate background knowledge.

    Answer A: We need to think of learning like a filing cabinet. We have a lot of information floating around in our heads. It is necessary to bring stored information from being "in" our minds to being "on" our minds in order to attach newly learned information to already known topics.

15. **Mark is planning a social studies lesson for his high school freshman on the 1920s. What would be the best activity for Mark to use to begin his lesson?**

    A. Students should read a short article about that includes the highlights of the 1920s.

    B. Students should work in small groups and brainstorm all the things they already know about the 1920s.

    C. Students should research a few key topics of the 1920s.

    D. Students should be introduced to some key vocabulary that is important in understanding the 1920s.

    Answer B: By listing what they already know about the 1920s students are activating prior knowledge about the topic so that they can attach newly learned information onto what they already know. This is a way to bring information that is "in" our minds to the forefront so that it is "on" our minds.

16. Mr. Henderson wants his students to know exactly what "comprehension" is so they can understand that when they read, they are not just reading the words, but understanding what the text is saying. What should Mr. Henderson do?

    A. Have students look up the word comprehension, write down its definition, and write a sentence explaining how comprehension and reading go together.

    B. He should have students write an essay about what comprehension is and why it is important in reading.

    C. Have students complete a word map for the word comprehension where they write its definition, determine some synonyms and antonyms, and determine three ways that they know it has occurred.

    D. Complete an acrostic poem using the word comprehension.

    Answer C: By investigating what comprehension means rather than just copying a definition out of the dictionary, students can truly understand what the word comprehension means.

17. **What is the purpose of using clustering or mind mapping activities in a lesson?**

    A. It helps students become more organized.

    B. Mind mapping and clustering is a great study skill that students can extend to their own independent study habits.

    C. It helps students organize large quantities of information in a visual or tactile-kinesthetic way.

    D. Mind mapping shows a teacher visually what a student is thinking mentally.

    Answer C: Our minds are like large filing cabinets and all of the information that we have is stored in chunks or clusters. Mind mapping activities allow us to visually see the information and organize it in a way so that our mind can easily categorize and process the information.

18. **What might be an explanation for why young children under the age of 2 put everything their mouths?**

    A. They are developing their sense of taste and they have not developed the knowledge that only food goes in your mouth.

    B. Their vocabulary develops faster if they are able to utilize the tongue muscle in various ways.

    C. Piaget says that children from birth to 2 are in the sensory motor stage and this is how children experience the world.

    D. Only kinesthetic-tactile learners do this. It is an early indicator of what type of learner a child will be.

    Answer C: Children go through many different stages as they grow up at various rates. It is common for two year olds to put things in their mouths. This does help them understand and acquaint themselves with the things around them and their environments.

19. **A young child in first grade is a struggling reader. What should the teacher do?**

    A. Refer the child for special education testing; she must have a learning disability.

    B. Continue to instruct the child at her instructional reading level. Learning is developmental and she may just not be developmentally where the other children are.

    C. Continue to monitor the student and pass her observations onto the second grade teacher next year.

    D. Have a discussion with the parents about what they should be doing at home to increase the student's reading achievements.

    Answer B: Children develop at different rates and this is very evident during the early elementary school years especially in reading where children will demonstrate a large variance in what they have mastered.

20. Mrs. Talmadge does not like her students to talk while they are working. She believes that the best learning occurs in a quiet, focused, on-task environment. She does not allow students to work cooperatively or in pairs. Students only complete learning activities individually. What does Mrs. Talmadge need to understand about the brain and how it best learns?

    A. The brain is social.

    B. The brain is a complex adaptive system.

    C. We use patterns to learn more effectively.

    D. Emotions are crucial to developing patterns.

    Answer A: Since the brain is social, it learns through communication and social interaction. If children are denied this useful learning tool, they will not learn as the brain was intended to.

21. At first glance it would appear that Ms. Marshall does not know how to manage her classroom because students in her class are standing over their desks, or tapping their pencils on their legs, and walking around the room at times. However, upon further examination, it is clear that Ms. Marshall's students are all on task and actively engaged in their learning. Ms. Marshal must embrace

    A. The constructivist approach to learning

    B. The multiple intelligence theory of interpersonal learning.

    C. The multiple intelligence theory of bodily/kinesthetic learning.

    D. The latest brain research and its importance toward learning.

    Answer C: Bodily kinesthetic learning says that students learn through movement and touch. This teacher clearly understands that students need to move in order to understand information.

22. **In which subject would students do much better if they were able to connect the learning to their own interests?**

    A. Physical Education

    B. Math

    C. Writing

    D. All of the above

    Answer D: It is proven that students learn best when new information pertains to their own lives and is relevant. This should occur across all disciplines.

23. **A 3rd grade teacher wants to integrate more critical thinking lessons into her day. Which of the lessons below will best incorporate critical thinking skills?**

    A. Doing some comparative shopping to find the better deal; 30% off each item purchased, or perhaps buy one get one free of a more expensive item.

    B. Writing how-to directions that students will then follow.

    C. Taking a field trip to reinforce what has been learned in the classroom.

    D. Brainstorming a list of newly learned concepts.

    Answer A: Critical thinking lessons are lessons that students might need in their daily lives. Percentages are a part of many student's everyday lives and they will find this skill very useful and will want to learn and master it.

24. **Which is the best example of a question that would be part of the synthesis segment on Bloom's Taxonomy?**

    A. When did Christopher Columbus set sail for the new world?

    B. How might Christopher Columbus' journey be different if it were to take place today?

    C. Which explorer do you think had the greatest impact on life as we know it today? Why?

    D. What were the names of Columbus' three ships?

    Answer B: Synthesizing requires students to take learned information and combine it with knowledge they already have and arrive at a conclusion. In this scenario, students take new information about Christopher Columbus and combine it with their knowledge about the world today to arrive at a conclusion.

25. **Bradley, a 10th grade student, has recently been getting poor grades in his English class. Bradley has always been a straight A student but is now receiving Cs and Ds consistently. What might be going on with Bradley?**

    A. Bradley probably needs glasses because he cannot see the words as easily as he used to be able to.

    B. Bradley no longer likes his English teacher and is doing poorly.

    C. Bradley has been playing basketball and it started a few months ago.

    D. Bradley probably has something going on at home like a divorce or neglect.

    Answer D: Students' grades don't normally drop for with no reason behind it. It is a teacher's responsibility to find out what might behind any drastic changes in student behavior.

26. **A teacher has a list of classroom rules posted that she made up prior to the beginning of the school year. She has reviewed them with the class, but they are having a difficult time following the rules that have been posted. What might the problem be?**

    A. The teacher must have a class full of students who have been diagnosed with ADHD.

    B. The students did not participate in putting the list of rules together so they do not feel any ownership of the expectations.

    C. The teacher didn't put the correct rules on her chart.

    D. The students don't know where the classroom rules are posted so they are unable to refer to them as needed.

    Answer B: When putting together a classroom list of rules, it is very important that the students participate in making that list of rules so they feel ownership over their classroom and what happens in it.

27. **Which would be an activity that might be seen in the success-oriented classroom?**

    A. A teacher has students working in collaborative pairs completing a Venn Diagram comparing two versions of the fairy tale *Cinderella.*

    B. Students are taking a multiple-choice test.

    C. A teacher is lecturing and students are diligently taking notes.

    D. Each student is reading a fairy tale and then they will discuss the differences between each story in small groups.

    Answer A: In a success-oriented classroom, mistakes are viewed as a natural part of the learning process. The tasks that are selected meet the needs of the student.

28. **A well-prepared reading lesson will include**

    A. lecture, note taking, and a quiz or test.

    B. a before, during, and after reading activity

    C. independent reading, paired reading, and independent seatwork

    D. a whole group activity based on a shared novel that everyone can discuss.

    Answer B: Any lesson will first activate background knowledge before the new lesson is presented, students will be active participants in a reading activity to increase comprehension, and then the teacher will assess student learning through an after activity.

29. **A kindergarten teacher evaluates a student's social skills while a student is in the writing center, at the play center, at a math center, and out on the playground for two weeks. Which method of social skill assessment is the teacher using?**

    A. Sociometric measures

    B. Teacher rating

    C. Role play

    D. Direct observation

    Answer D: Direct observation is when a teacher observes a student in various settings with a checklist.

30. **Mr. Anderson plays kickball with his class every Friday at recess. What important skill is Mr. Anderson teaching his students during this time?**

    A. A great math lesson on how to keep score.

    B. A physics lesson on the trajectory of the ball when kicked a certain way.

    C. The value of being on a team and playing together fairly.

    D. How to follow directions to play a fair game.

    Answer C: One way to teach social skills is through play and peer interaction. By playing kickball with his class, Mr. Anderson can also serve as a role model for correct behaviors when one is part of a team.

31. **A teacher has 85 middle school students that she is responsible for. She has a bin for each of her classes that she calls the "done bin". This management strategy most likely**

    A. Does not help students because they want to hand their papers to the teacher directly.

    B. Allows students to look at each other's papers.

    C. Distracting to students because they forget to put their papers in the correct bin.

    D. helpful to students because they always know where to put their papers when they have completed their work

    Answer D: Effective teachers deal with daily classroom procedures efficiently and quickly because then students will spend the majority of class time engaged in academic tasks, which will likely result in higher achievement. By knowing where their papers are supposed to go, students don't waste a lot of time waiting for the teacher to come and collect their things. In addition, the papers are more likely not to get lost or misplaced by the students.

32. **Before lunch a teacher lines her classroom up by the row that they sit in. This is an example of**

    A. a proactive strategy

    B. a transitional interference

    C. a waste of time and inefficient

    D. a transition signal

    Answer A: Early in the year, the teacher pinpoints the transition periods in the day and anticipates possible behavior problems. By lining up by row, the teacher knows that lining everyone up at once could be a problem.

33. **When a fourth grade teacher wants to get the attention of her students, she raises her hand and smiles. Students then do the same when they notice her until everyone in the class is doing the same thing. This is an example of**

    A. a proactive strategy

    B. a transition signal

    C. a waste of time that students will not understand

    D. a transitional interference

    Answer B: A transition signal is a teacher utterance or gesture that indicates movement of the lesson from one topic or activity to another by indicating where the lesson is and where it is going. By getting students attention first, the teacher knows when the class is ready to receive the next direction.

34. **A teacher's room is so cold one day that her classes must take place in a different location for the day. What is something that the teacher should take a few moments to do?**

    A. Tell kids to wear warmer clothes tomorrow in case their room is just as cold the next day.

    B. Put a note on her regular classroom door indicating where they are for the day.

    C. Report the problem to maintenance and have them fix the temperature gauge immediately.

    D. Become familiar with the evacuation routes for this particular room and share these plans with the students.

    Answer D: You never know when a crisis is going to happen and if a teacher changes locations for the day, she should take the time to make everyone familiar with what needs to be done should an emergency arise.

35. **A state's curriculum says that in the first quarter students should learn summarizing, making connections to text, and using context clues while reading. This is the**

    A. scope

    B. sequence

    C. outline

    D. curriculum alignment

    Answer B: Sequence is the outline of what should be taught before and after a particular subject. The curriculum here states what should be taught first, second, third, and fourth.

36. **At the beginning of each school year it is a good idea for the teacher to**

    A. use the exit tests from the prior year to determine the abilities of their new students.

    B. place students in groups and evaluate how they do and rearrange groups accordingly.

    C. give a diagnostic assessment to determine students' abilities.

    D. talk to their student's prior year teachers to determine their ability levels.

    Answer C: A diagnostic assessment determines individual weaknesses and strengths in specific areas. It is a good idea to get to know your students by giving a diagnostic assessment at the beginning of the year to assist with grouping.

37. **A teacher is teaching time to her second grade students. The best way that she can differentiate is to**

    A. teach one group time, one group multiplication, and one group division.

    B. have one group use technology to learn time and the other to use paper pencil method.

    C. break students into groups and have them all complete the same task.

    D. determine which students need practice with time to the various hours, which group needs time to the 5 minutes, and which group needs to learn time to the minute.

    Answer D: There are three primary ways to differentiate: content, process, and product. This example differentiates the content that is presented to different groups of students based on individual needs.

38. **Students are given a choice between 3 final projects to complete after reading a group novel. How has the teacher chosen to differentiate?**

    A. Product

    B. Process

    C. Content

    D. This is not an example of differentiation.

    Answer A: Product differentiation is the result of learning. Usually, a product is the result or assessment of learning. In this example, students have a choice of how they are going to show what they have learned.

39. **A 10th grade teacher has presented her class of sophomores with a scientific scenario dealing with a problem in their school that they must solve. Four groups have been given different, but related scenarios to discuss. The teacher has**

    A. Differentiated instruction

    B. Used cooperative learning models

    C. Provided a relevant learning experience

    D. All of the above

    Answer D: Since the teacher has given different groups of students various scenarios, she has differentiated the lesson. The groups each have a relevant problem to solve together and discuss which is an example of cooperative learning. Since the problem has to do with the students' school, it is relevant.

40. **What does the quote, "Assessment drives instruction, "mean?**

    A. Assessment must be a part of every instructional model.

    B. The results of any given assessment should be the determining factors of the next step of instruction.

    C. Standardized assessment test results should drive the foundation for the development of curriculum.

    D. Different methods of assessment should be used to vary presentation of material to students.

    Answer B: The reason that teachers assess is to see what students have mastered in a given topic. If they have not mastered the objectives taught, then it is a telling sign for the teacher of what needs to be taught again.

41. **A teacher wants to give her students a pretest before teaching them fractions so that she can plan her instruction effectively and group students according to their ability. What kind of assessment should the teacher give as a pretest?**

    A. A project based assessment.

    B. An anecdotal record.

    C. A formal test

    D. A portfolio assessment

    Answer C: A formalized test will provide various comparative norms and scales for the assessment instrument. Therefore, the teacher can gain comparative information about the students' abilities and plan instruction accordingly.

42. **An English teacher needs to determine certain reading behaviors that her students possess. Which is the best type of assessment for her to give?**

    A. Anecdotal records.

    B. Formal standardized tests

    C. Rating scale or checklist.

    D. Portfolio assessment

    Answer A: Anecdotal records are notes recorded by the teacher concerning an area of interest or concern with particular students. Anecdotal records will give the teacher information about her students, recorded in her own words and observed with her own eyes.

43. **A teacher wants to know her student's feelings about a project they just completed; each student needed to create a commercial about their favorite book that they had read as a class. Which is the best method of assessment for the teacher to use?**

    A. Standardized test

    B. Portfolio assessment

    C. Rating scale and checklist

    D. Questioning

    Answer C: Rating scale and checklist assessments are generally self-appraisal instruments completed by the students. The focus of these is frequently on behavior or effective areas such as interest and motivation.

44. **How can questioning be used as a powerful assessment tool?**

    A. The students answer questions that are generated by the teacher.

    B. The students generate assessment questions to ask each other.

    C. The teacher questions students and collects a lot of valuable information.

    D. Open ended written questions will tell a teacher a lot more about student knowledge than will oral questioning.

    Answer C: As the teacher orally questions students daily, she collects a great deal of information about the degree of student learning and potential sources of confusion for the students. Therefore, it is a powerful assessment tool for teachers.

45. **Kellough and Roberts feel that students should be evaluated on**

    A. What the learner says

    B. What the learner does

    C. What the learner.

    D. All of the above.

    Answer D: Thorndike has identified three types of assessment: standardized tests, assessment material packaged with curricular materials, teacher-made assessment instruments. Kellough and Roberts have a different view. They feel that students should be assessed by what a student says, does, and writes. They believe that this is a more authentic assessment model.

46. **What is the best method for teaching social skills within the classroom?**

    A. Standardized testing

    B. Heterogeneous grouping methods

    C. Teacher role modeling

    D. Student role playing

    Answer C: Since the teacher is the adult in charge of the students each and every day, they have an awesome responsibility of being good role models. Teachers need to remember the saying, "do as I do, not as I say".

47. **A second grade teacher has four reading groups named after various birds. This teacher uses**

    A. group fragmentation

    B. management transition

    C. transition signals

    D. seat work

    Answer A: Smooth transitions occur when students move in groups or clusters rather than one by one. This is the idea behind group fragmentation and that is what the teacher in this scenario has done.

48. **Which teacher probably has an easier time managing her students' transitions?**

    A. A teacher whose daily schedule is different every day.

    B. A teacher who tells her students what to expect each day.

    C. A teacher whose daily schedule is consistent each day.

    D. A teacher who has taught elementary school before and now teach middle school.

    Answer C: Children thrive on consistency and structure. The teacher who has a schedule that is consistent from day to day will be more successful because her students know exactly what to expect and what will be coming next.

49. **Which of the following does not factor into invitational learning?**

    A. A well lit classroom.

    B. A temperature controlled classroom.

    C. A calming atmosphere.

    D. Proximity to resource classrooms and the cafeteria.

    Answer D: Invitational learning is a theory of learning that centers on adequate, well-built, and well-equipped classrooms that invite students to learn. The proximity to resource classrooms and the cafeteria doesn't have any bearing on whether students will learn or not.

50. **What is the proper way to prepare for a tornado?**

    A. Have students remain at their seats with their heads down.

    B. Have students clear of any windows and have them crouch down on the floor and cover their heads with their hands.

    C. Exit outside using the closest exits.

    D. All students should convene in the gymnasium until any dangerous weather has passed.

    Answer B: Choice B is the universal way to prepare for a tornado in an educational institution and should be practiced in drills at every educational institution.

51. It is necessary for 4th grade students to learn multiplication and division before they can be introduced to reducing fractions. This criteria is known as the curriculum

    A. Sequence

    B. Scope

    C. Design

    D. Instruction

    Answer A: Sequence is the order in which things occur. Students must learn multiplication and division before they can learn about reducing fractions since multiplication and division are necessary operations in order to reduce fractions.

52. What is the best reason for giving a pre-test in math?

    A. The teacher needs to let the students know what they are going to learn about in an upcoming unit.

    B. The teacher needs to know if students are ready to learn new material.

    C. It will help the teacher differentiate instruction during the unit.

    D. You can compare students' prior knowledge to how they do on the final assessment.

    Answer C: A teacher must get to know students' abilities and knowledge on a topic before she teaches it. This information can be gained by giving a pretest. By only teaching students what they do not already know, a teacher can gain a lot of valuable instructional time.

53. **A teacher makes a final exam for her English Literature class that includes some multiple choice and short answer questions. What type of assessment has the teacher created?**

    A. A formal test

    B. An informal test

    C. An anecdotal record

    D. A portfolio assessment

    Answer B: Since the test has not been standardized using a large sample population. Therefore, it is considered an informal test.

54. **As a form of assessment to use on her report cards, a teacher keeps notes on observed behaviors of her students during guided reading groups. What type of assessment is this an example of?**

    A. Formal assessment

    B. Informal assessment

    C. Portfolio assessment

    D. Anecdotal records

    Answer D: Anecdotal records are notes recorded by the teacher concerning an area of interest of concern with a particular student. In this case, the teacher is using the information to alert parents to a student's progress on their report cards.

55. **A student and a teacher are sitting down together and deciding which pieces of student work to keep to document the student's progress. This is an example of which type of assessment?**

    A. Rating scales and checklists

    B. Anecdotal records

    C. Portfolio assessment

    D. Questioning

    Answer C: A collection of work compiled over an extended time period allows teacher, student, and parents to view the student's progress from a unique perspective. This is an example of portfolio assessment.

56. **Which assessment tool gives teachers a great deal of information on a daily basis?**

    A. Questioning

    B. Anecdotal records

    C. Formal assessments

    D. Portfolio assessments

    Answer A: Questioning doesn't require any preparation. Teachers can ask meaningful questions on the fly and gain valuable information about student progress.

57. **Why might a school use Criterion-referenced assessments?**

    A. To make sure that the content schools are teaching students applies to real-world needs.

    B. To document and measure whether schools are making AYP (Annual Yearly Progress) as documented in No Child Left Behind.

    C. To rank students for differentiated instruction within the school.

    D. To rate schools for state funding.

    Answer B: Criterion-referenced assessments are tools that examine specific student learning goals and performance compared to a norm group of student learners. To measure for AYP, a school needs to compare their own performance to the normal performance of students across the country.

58. **Why might a school use Norm-referenced assessments?**

    A. To make sure that the content schools are teaching students applies to real world needs.

    B. To document and measure whether schools are making AYP (Annual Yearly Progress) as documented in No Child Left Behind.

    C. To rank students for differentiated instruction within the school.

    D. To rate schools for state funding.

    Answer C: Norm-referenced tests are tools used to classify student learners for homogenous groupings based on ability levels or basic skills into a ranking category. Sometimes it is necessary to see if students are performing above or below the norm.

59. **The DRA is a direct reading assessment tool used by many schools across the country. Teachers listen to students read and determine the miscues they are making while they read, but it also asks the student to use reading strategies and read strategically for comprehension. What type of assessment is the DRA?**

    A. Summative assessment

    B. Placement assessment

    C. Interest and attitude assessment

    D. Diagnostic assessment

    Answer D: Diagnostic assessments determine individual weakness and strengths in specific areas. The DRA assessment measures a student's strengths and weaknesses in the area of reading.

60. **Two fourth grade teachers share students for math. Before each unit of study each teacher gives her class a pretest. What type of assessment is this?**

    A. Readiness assessment

    B. Interest and attitude assessment

    C. Evaluation assessment

    D. Placement assessment

    Answer D: Placement assessments are used for grouping students or determining appropriate beginning levels in leveled materials. In this case the teacher can determine at what level the students should be instructed based on the results of the test.

61. **What was the purpose of the No Child Left Behind Act passed in 2001?**

    A. It was an act passed as a way to ensure that all children passed a standardized assessment before being passed on to the next grade.

    B. To mandate a set amount of funds to schools that did a good job of educating their students.

    C. It aims to improve schools by increasing educational standards and holds schools, school districts, and states accountable for performance and progress of students.

    D. It allows parents to choose which school their child attends by using vouchers.

    Answer C: The No Child Left Behind Act was passed in 2001 to improve schools by increasing educational standards and holding schools, school districts, and states accountable for performance and progress of students.

62. **What are magnet schools?**

    A. Schools that attract a certain demographic of student.

    B. Schools that are built around the regular education building.

    C. Schools that are available for any student within the district. These schools usually have a theme.

    D. Schools that are not run by the school districts but take money, based on student enrollment, from the local public school.

    Answer C: Usually magnet schools have themes such as business academics or college preparatory curricula. Magnet schools want to captivate students by teaching to what they are most interested in.

63. **There are many professional organizations for teachers to join in New York state at the local or national level. What is the advantage of teachers joining a professional organization?**

    A. It is a great way for teachers to become well-known in their field.

    B. Joining a professional organization is a great way to reduce a teacher's tax base.

    C. Professional organizations are the only way to get up-to-date teaching information about a discipline because state organizations have better information than the districts do.

    D. By joining a professional organization, a teacher can network with other educators outside of their own school or district and gain valuable teaching ideas and information.

    Answer D: The profession of teaching tends to be very isolated since teachers do not have a lot of time to socialize and converse with other professionals. By joining a professional organization, a teacher is carving out time to meet and learn from other teachers.

64. **Math teachers K-8 in a district are using the same math program from the same publisher. How was this decision most likely made?**

    A. K-8 teachers got together and looked over several different math programs/models and decided that the one they are using is the best one to use.

    B. Most likely it was a centralized decision by the district central office and the math program was used to ensure consistency across grades K-8.

    C. Parents of the district got together and decided that the math program the district is using is the best one for their children.

    D. Each individual school decided to use the current math program because it was the best one for their individual schools.

    Answer B: Centralized decision making is when a large entity, like the federal government or even the state government, makes the decision that will affect all the smaller groups – like local schools. In this example, the entity that made the decision is central office and the decision affects all k-8 schools in a district.

65. **What is the responsibility of the New York State Board of Regents?**

    A. This group is the chief officer of the school district,

    B. A sixteen member group that presides over the NYSED and develops guidelines, creates and monitors aid, and develops policies.

    C. It is a collective bargaining organization.

    D. It allows small school districts to combine their financial power to share costs.

    Answer B: The New York State Board of Regents are elected by the state legislature, and are responsible for the general supervision of all educational activities in the state. They preside over the New York State Education Department.

66. **A teacher has just finished teaching a lesson about the branches of government. As she is reviewing the grades of her students for the unit, she is also reviewing what worked well and didn't work well. What is the teacher doing when she asks herself these questions?**

    A. Grading the students.

    B. Deciding if the unit is worth teaching next year.

    C. Self-assessing and reflecting on how to improve her teaching the next time she teaches the unit.

    D. Determining the content that needs to be added to the unit next time in order for her students to master the material.

    Answer C: Self-assessing and reflection are important aspects of the teaching profession. A teacher that no longer, or never did, reflect on their own performance is no longer growing, improving, or changing as a professional.

67. **A science teacher realizes that one of his weaknesses is showing his students how to read the textbook to improve understanding. What is something the teacher might consider doing?**

    A. He should take a course on science and the standardized testing methods used to evaluate students in his state.

    B. He should attend some professional development opportunities that address teaching students to comprehend non-fiction text.

    C. He should speak with the English teacher on his team and have them work a little more with comprehending non-fiction material.

    D. He should find a textbook that is below the students' grade level that they can easily understand and focus on the content rather than the decoding while they read.

    Answer B: If this teacher did attend some professional development opportunities on teaching students how to read non-fiction texts, he is continuing to grow and develop as an educator and is doing his future students a great favor.

68. **A local middle school English grade level department meets every Wednesday with their subject matter peers. They call this meeting a PLC (Primary Learning Community). What is most likely the purpose of these PLCs?**

    A. The PLC allows teachers to learn from each other and share successful lessons they have used in their classrooms.

    B. It is a chance for teachers review and change student's IEPs.

    C. PLCs are the first step before a CST meeting.

    D. The meeting gives these teachers a chance to review curriculum and discuss changes that must be made to meet the needs of their students.

    Answer A: Since the teaching profession is known for being very individualized and isolated, a PLC is very important in establishing continuity within a school, department, and grade level. It also gives teachers a chance to talk and communicate about what is going on in their own classroom as well as gain valuable information about what is going on in other classrooms.

69. **A new 4th grade teacher has been hired and this is her first year teaching. What is the best thing that the district or school can do to make this teacher's first year successful?**

    A. Have this new hire attend an orientation that will orient the new teacher to the practices and policies of the county.

    B. Supply her with several books about being a new teacher and what other teachers have done to successfully make it through the first year.

    C. Observe her classroom more often than a veteran teacher and offer constructive criticism on ways to improve instruction and management within her classroom and make reports to central office on her performance.

    D. Assign a mentor teacher to her so she can ask for professional teaching advice in the areas she is struggling in.

    Answer D: Part of being an effective teacher is to not only have students grow educationally, but to allow oneself to also continue to grow as a teacher. Working with other members of the school community – peers, supervisors, and other staff – will give the teacher the necessary grounding needed to increase skills and knowledge sets.

70. **It is the second month of school and a teacher has received several emails from one parent in particular. What should the teacher do?**

    A. Ignore the parent's contacts that are not well justified.

    B. Do everything the parent suggests. After all, the parent knows their child better than the teacher.

    C. Respond politely to the parent telling them that she will take their thoughts into consideration and consult with their mentor teacher about how to handle the situation.

    D. Alert the principal and have them meet with the parent so that they will stop harassing the teacher.

    Answer C: As with any conflict that might arise in life, one must keep their cool and respond politely. Especially in the professional environment a teacher must handle parents with respect.

71. **A 2nd grade parent complains to a teacher that he does not feel that the teacher is communicating well with the parents. What is one way that the teacher can increase communication with her students' parents?**

    A. The teacher can send a weekly newsletter informing parents of the classroom activities for that week and the week to come.

    B. The teacher can call parents of children who were difficult that week or had a great week.

    C. The teacher can invite parents into the classroom to help out more often.

    D. The teacher can invite parents to holiday parties so that they feel they are a part of the classroom.

    Answer A: Newsletters are particularly effective in informing families of what is going on in the classroom. A weekly newsletter is a great way to communicate with parents.

72. **A teacher is having a conference with a parent tomorrow. She has records of student behavior and has the notes that she has been keeping about the child's classroom behaviors and performance. What else would be helpful for the teacher to have handy before the conference?**

    A. The principal should also attend to give the teacher support.

    B. Another grade level teacher should attend to give the teacher support.

    C. The child should also be at the conference so they can defend their position.

    D. Samples of student work and models of exemplary work should be available to support the teacher's position.

    Answer D: It is great for parents to see examples of exemplary work from other students in the class so they can compare their child's work with the exemplary work of others. A teacher must remember to remove the name from the exemplary work however in order to keep confidentiality.

73. **What is one of the benefits of having students work with an adult mentor?**

    A. The student will learn how to be a mature, responsible adult.

    B. The student will learn about diversity and respect for their elders.

    C. The student is exposed to multicultural education and feels a sense of personalized instruction.

    D. It takes some of the responsibility of education off the teacher's and parent's shoulders. After all, it takes a village.

    Answer C: Adult mentors work individually with identified students on specific subject areas to reinforce the learning through tutorial instruction and application of knowledge. Using adult mentors helps to increase or maximize student learning beyond the classroom.

74. **Mrs. Montgory's class has several students who are reading below grade level. However, the families of these students also cannot afford to have a private tutor. Mrs. Montgory cannot give any more time to help these students individually. What would be the best solution to help these struggling students receive more individualized attention?**

   A. Mrs. Montgory can pay for the private tutor herself.

   B. The librarian can work with the students individually during library time each week.

   C. Mrs. Montgory can work with retired community members to come in and read with students a few times a week on a volunteer basis.

   D. The parents must be given a strict schedule to follow at home in order to assist with improving their child's reading.

   Answer C: Sometimes all children need is a little extra attention from another adult to excel in a certain subject. Especially in the area of reading, students might just need a little extra time to practice with a knowledgeable adult in order to improve simply because they do not have the support at home, or just simply need more time to focus on a particular subject.

75. **What will students gain by having community members involved in the classroom and the school?**

   A. Students will learn how to interact with adults.

   B. Students will experience accountability and responsibility.

   C. Students will see what it is like to be a community leader.

   D. Students will learn to set goals to improve their performance in school with adult intervention.

   Answer B: Students will be more accountable for their work and will feel a greater responsibility toward their learning.

76. **What is usually the teacher's role when a student has been referred to a CST for evaluation?**

    A. The work is extensive for a teacher because they are given strict guidelines to follow within the classroom over several weeks.

    B. Teachers are asked to make observations and report to the team in about a week.

    C. There is usually a little paperwork for teachers to fill out and some in-class observations of a student.

    D. The classroom teacher doesn't have any responsibility. Referring and evaluating a student is the specialists' responsibility.

    Answer C: Since the teacher is the school employee who has the most contact with a student, they normally have to fill out a little paperwork about the child's behavior and work habits. They also will have to make some classroom observations and modifications for the child to see if any classroom changes will help the child improve.

77. **Does a parent have to be involved in a child's IEP?**

    A. Yes

    B. No

    C. Only under certain circumstances.

    D. It is optional.

    Answer A: Yes, a parent must sign off on the goals set forth for a child in an IEP and must be part of the IEP meeting and goal setting process.

78. **What is the least restrictive environment under IDEA?**

    A. A law that says that disabled students cannot be restrained by teachers or assistants.

    B. The mandate that children be educated to the maximum extent appropriate with their non-disabled peers.

    C. A modification that sometimes appears in student's IEPs.

    D. A policy where disabled students can be placed in the regular classroom, as long as such placement does not interfere with the student's educational plan.

    Answer B: Usually, the regular education classroom is thought to be the least restrictive environment for any learning disabled children.

79. **What is mainstreaming?**

    A. A policy where disabled students can be placed in the regular classroom, as long as such placement does not interfere with the student's educational plan.

    B. A law that says that disabled students can not be restrained by teachers or assistants.

    C. A way of teaching in the classroom that ensures that all students are taught the same way across the curriculum.

    D. The mandate that children be educated to the maximum extent appropriate with their non-disabled peers.

    Answer A: Students who do not have any disabilities are known as the main stream of students. Under IDEA, students with disabilities are to be included in the main stream of students as often as possible.

80. **A teacher has a student that wears the same dirty sweatshirt to class each day, never has a lunch, and claims that he lives in a closet. What should the teacher do?**

    A. Nothing.

    B. Be the best teacher she can to this poor student.

    C. Report the potential neglect situation to authorities; she is mandated by law to.

    D. See if she has any clothes at home that would fit this student and pass them on to him.

    Answer C: If a teacher suspects abuse – whether it be physical, emotional, or neglect, they are mandated by law to report their feelings.

www.ingramcontent.com/pod-product-compliance
Lightning Source LLC
LaVergne TN
LVHW061316060426
835507LV00019B/2178